The Faery Tea Party Cook Book

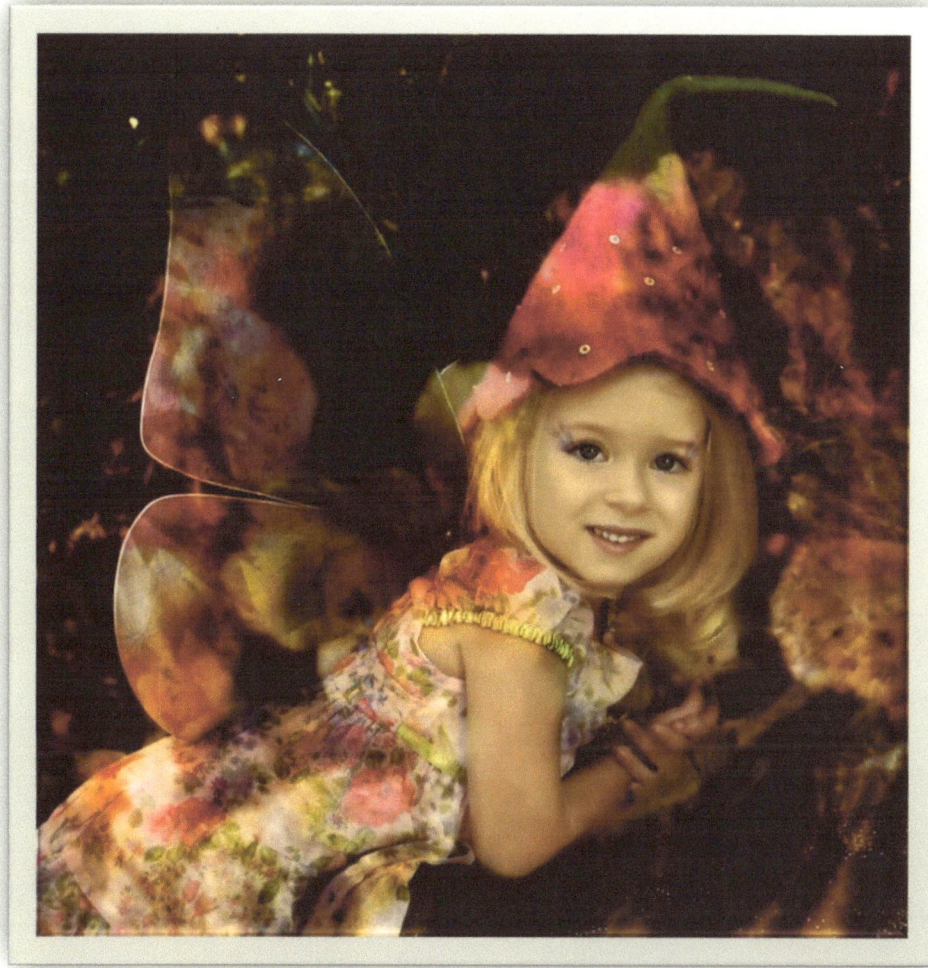

By Linda Larson

The Faery Tea Party Cook Book

By Linda Larson

Faery Photography by Jacqueline Underwood

www.UnderwoodPhoto.com
www.Fae-Entertainment.ca

First published by Fae Entertainment Flights of Fantasy

ISBN# 978-0-9917470-6-1

This book is printed and available in Kindle, eBook and Paperback Worldwide.

Apple or Plum Faery Crumble

12 Large Apples, peeled, cored
8 oz. Brown Sugar
1oz. Cinnamon
1 pinch Nutmeg
12 oz. Flour
1 oz. Salt
1/ Lb. Butter, melted

Preheat oven to 180°. Peel, core, and thinly slice the apples into a large bowl. Spoon the apples or plums into a large buttered deep-sided baking pan. Sift and mix the flour, salt, sugar, cinnamon and nutmeg into the bowl. Add the melted butter. Stir to make a crumble mixture, and pour over the apples or plums mixture. Bake in a preheated oven at 180° for 40 to 45 minutes, or until the sponge topping has risen and is browned. Serve hot with your choice of Devon-shire cream, Whipped Cream or Vanilla Ice Cream. Enjoy a Faery delicious dessert, and use any fruit to make this Faerielicious Crumble with a wave of your Faery magic wand!

Do you love Brambleberries?

Brambleberry Faery Scones

16 oz. Flour
1 oz. Sugar
½ oz. Baking Powder
½ oz. Salt
2 Lbs.. Butter (room temperature)
1 oz. Orange zest
150 ml. Buttermilk
2.5 ml. Vanilla Extract
1 Egg
4 oz. Milk
2 oz. Brown Sugar
1 Lb. Frozen Brambleberries (do not over-mix)

In a large mixing bowl sift the flour, sugar, baking powder, and salt ingredients together. Mix the butter in with a spatula until the batter resembles small crumb consistency. Add the orange zest, buttermilk and frozen brambleberries (or blackberries) making sure that you stir very gently as to not break the berries up too much (be careful not to over mix). Gently place small dollops for your scones onto a parchment lined baking sheet molding them into rounds or triangles. Brush the tops with the beaten egg/milk mixture (for making the scones a golden brown top during baking). Bake in a preheated 200° oven for 15 minutes until risen and golden brown in color. You can serve this with a choice of Devonshire cream, Whipped Cream or Ice Cream on the side. Yummy Favorite Faery Food!

Apple Brambleberry Faery Pandowdy Cobbler

6 large Apples, peeled and cored
1 Lb. Brambleberries
½ Lb. Sugar
1 oz. Cinnamon
1 pinch Nutmeg
8 oz. Flour
1 pinch Salt
1 oz. Baking Powder
¼ Lb. Butter, melted
 4 oz. Milk

Peel, core, and thinly slice the apples into a large bowl. Add the brambleberries (or blackberries), half of the sugar, cinnamon, nutmeg, and gently stir apples and berries together until evenly coated. Spoon the mixture into a large buttered deep-sided baking pan. Sift and mix the flour, salt, baking powder and sugar into the bowl. Add the melted butter and the milk. Stir to make a smooth batter, and pour over the apple-brambleberry mixture. Bake in a preheated oven at 180° for 40 to 45 minutes, or until the sponge topping has risen and is browned. Serve hot with your choice of Devon- shire cream, whipped cream or ice cream. Enjoy a very delicious dessert, and use any fruit to make this delectable pandowdy!

Exquisite Faery Tea

Irish or English Tea Leafs, loose leafs
Tea Strainers for cups
Lemons, sliced
Sugar Cubes
Whole Milk
Honey

Additions for refreshing iced tea;

Fresh Raspberries
Fresh Mint Leafs

Boil water in a large tea kettle on the stove, and pour water into a tea pot to pre-warm the tea pot ahead of time. Then, re-boil some more water for the actual tea water to be steeped. Have your table set out with cups, tea strainers on top of the cups, and separate spoons, lemons, sugar cubes, whole milk and honey. Pour the first batch of boiled water out of the tea pot, and add 2 Teaspoons of fresh loose tea leafs into the warm tea pot. Then, pour the second batch of boiled tea water into the tea pot, and let it steep for 3 to 6 minutes. Gently stir your tea before serving, pouring it through the strainers into each cup. Serve with your choice of lemon, sugar, whole milk, or honey added. If you are serving this tea in the summertime, then let the strained tea cool in the refrigerator after adding some fresh mint leafs and sugar or honey to taste for at least two hours before serving. Add a few raspberries to the chilled tea while serving in a clear tea cup. Your guests will be pleasantly surprised at the lovely mixture of delicate flavors to please their palate. For children, you can use a decaffeinated tea, and make sure tea is never served to hot for them to drink. Enjoy, and serve with scones, Devonshire cream, jams, tea biscuits, cakes, fresh fruit, cucumber sandwiches and fresh fruits. What a crowd pleaser! All your Faery guests will love this exquisite Old English Faery Tea!

Faery Scrumptious Bread Pudding

1 Box instant Vanilla Pudding or Custard
Milk added to Pudding, mixed to use
1 oz. Lemon Zest
½ Lb. Currants or Frozen Blueberries
Pinch Nutmeg
½ oz. Cinnamon
12 Slices Bread, crust cut off
4 oz. Apricot Jam
 2 oz. Water
2 oz. Whipped Cream
5 ml. Butter

Rub the 2 teaspoons of Butter into a deep dish baking pan, and sprinkle with some flour to keep the pudding from sticking to surface during baking. Line the baking pan with the pieces of bread covering the entire surface, including the sides of the pan as far up as possible. Pre-make your pudding or custard, add the cinnamon and nutmeg, and set aside covered in a refrigerator to use later. Bake the bread in a preheated oven for 8 minutes on 170° until the bread is very lightly toasted. Remove from oven. In a separate saucepan, warm the jam and water until honey-syrup consistency. Spread the jam sauce evenly over the toasted bread, pour the pudding over the layered jam, and top off with a layer of whipped cream. Chill for one hour, and serve in dessert compote dishes with a sprig of fresh mint and a dusting of powdered sugar for an extra sweet zing. A Faery dreamy dish!

Faery Cucumber Sandwiches

Sliced Fresh White Bread
1 cube Soft Butter
1 English Cucumber, thinly sliced
Salt & Pepper to taste
Watercress (optional)

Butter one side of each piece of bread, placing 1 layer of overlapping cucumber slices on top of the buttered surface. Lightly salt and pepper. Place another buttered slice of bread, butter side down onto the sliced cucumber layer. Trim off bread crusts and cut diagonally into quarters. For an authentic Faery Cucumber Sandwiches, add leaves of Watercress on top of the sliced Cucumbers. Deliciously Faery elegant with your favorite Faery treats at tea time.

Faeries are so Happy

In The Moon Shine,

And In The Sun Rise...

As the Faeries

Watch the Sun Set

They will gather their feast,

Eat, chew,

And digest...

Once again,

They will become hungry -

And then The Sun will Rise...

Empty...

They will fill back up again

This is why

Faeries Are So Happy-

Faery Buttermilk Biscuit Scones

1 Lb. Flour
8 full oz. Buttermilk
3 oz. melted butter
1/2 oz. Salt
2 oz. of Baking Soda

For a Berry scone, add fresh fruit to the dough before baking. Mix flour with buttermilk to form thick dough. Cover and leave in a warm place for 12 to 24 hours. Add remaining ingredients and mix dough thoroughly. Roll dough out about ¾ inch thick onto a floured surface. Cut biscuits using a floured butter knife, cut diagonally into triangles and place on a buttered baking sheet. Bake for 40 minutes at 180°. Serve hot with butter. Devonshire Cream makes a great addition to these lovely delectable Faerielicious yummy Buttermilk Scones! A Faery treat delightful enough for a dreamy Faery to dream big dreams!

Brambleberry Faery Pie

2 unbaked Pastry Pie Crusts
2 Lbs. Brambleberries
1-2 large Apple(s)
1 Lb. Sugar
2 Tablespoons Butter
1 oz. Lemon rind
Juice of 1 Lemon
2 Eggs

Put 2 Lbs. brambleberries and 1/2 apple into the pie shell. In a separate double saucepan, put the remaining 1 cup of brambleberries and 1/2 apple, cook, crush and simmer until soft. Sieve out and put pulp, beaten eggs, butter and grated lemon grind and juice back into the double saucepan. Heat and sire until thick. Pour over the brambleberry pie, cover with the remaining pie shell, seal the pie shell at edges, make four to six slits in the top of the pastry shell and bake at 190° until pastry is delicately browned (25 to 35 minutes) depending on the heat of your individual oven. If you use a thinner pie pastry crust, it may take less time for baking and browning. Serve hot with a scoop of Vanilla Ice Cream or a dollop of Devonshire Cream.

Never Fail Faery Pastry Pie Crust

Mix - 2 Lbs. Shortening or Butter
1 Lb. Flour (sifted)
½ oz. Baking Powder
Pinch of Salt
Beat - 1 Egg in a measuring cup
Add - 1 ½ oz. Vinegar, and then fill cup with 2 oz. mark cold water

Put all the ingredients together and mix well. Shape in a roll and store in refrigerator. This amount makes 3 large or 4 small two-crusted pastry pies. After crust is chilled, cut dough into 6 or 8 pieces, and roll into rounds with rolling pin. Fill bottom shell in pie tin, and fill with fruit filling, cover with top of pie crust, seal the edges and make small slits in the top of the pie shell for ventilation of steam while baking.

19

Brambleberry Faery Curd

1 Lb. Brambleberries
2 Eggs
1 green Apple
8oz. Sugar
Juice of 1 Lemon
4 oz. Butter

Put brambleberries and apple in saucepan and cook, crush and simmer until soft. Sieve and put pulp, beaten eggs, butter and grated lemon rind and juice in double saucepan. Heat and stir until thick. Add whole brambleberries at the end for texture. Pot and keep no longer than two months for freshness.

Faery Snow's a Fallin'

A tingle Lin...

Faery Snows a fallin'

Counting snowflakes,

A stratosphere in white...

Show me a numbering

Of how many sides I must count

Before it falls and does melt...

Mouth open...shivering-

It's Faery snow a fallin'

And I lost count!

Elderflower Fairy LACE

Faery Frivolous

LACE...

Lace to cover

The forest floor,

And Faery Party Flavors-

Faery Hugs,

And Hearts Awry

A Time Forgotten

A Time Surpassed

A Faery Arrival...

A Gift from the Past

Lovely Elderflower LACE

And Faery Fineness

Elderflower Fairy Cordial Champagne

1 Gallon Water
1 oz. White Wine Vinegar
1 Lemon Rind and Juice
7-10 Flavor Heads of Elderflower
1 ½ Lbs. White Sugar

Put flowers in a bowl and add lemon juice and rind (no pith), sugar and vinegar. Add cold water and leave covered with light cheesecloth for 24 hours. Strain and bottle into screw tops or empty champagne bottle with air tight cork. Leave for one to two weeks. Only fill 3/4 full, and screw tops on tightly. This is a non-alcoholic fizzy cordial refreshing spritz.

Apple Faery Plum Chutney

1 Lb. Finely Chopped Apples (peeled and cored)
1 Lb. Finely Chopped Plums (cored)
1 pint Malt Vinegar
1 oz. Salt
2 oz. yellow Raisins, chopped
1/2 Lb. Brown Sugar
2 Garlic Cloves, finely minced
1oz. ground Ginger
1 oz. Cinnamon
1 oz. Mustard Seed

Put vinegar and plums in a pan and crush. Simmer for 30 minutes and sieve. Put with apples, raisins, garlic, spice and salt. Bring to boil, add sugar and cook for 30 minutes. Stir in one teaspoon of mustard seed. Bottle and store in a cool place.

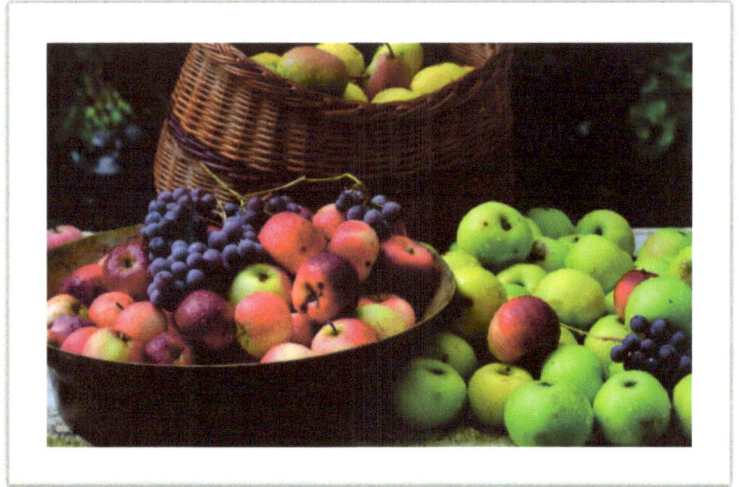

Apple Brambleberry Faery Jam

3 1/2 Lbs. of Apples
1 cup Water
2 Lbs. Brambleberries
3 1/2 Lbs. of Sugar
2 oz.. clear Gelatin (2 packages)

Peel, core apples and put into pan with a teacup of water. Simmer until tender. Add brambleberries and boil for 5 minutes before adding the sugar. Then boil well for 15-20 minutes. Add gelatin, stir well for 2 minutes. Let simmer on low heat for 10 minutes. Remove from heat, and enjoy!

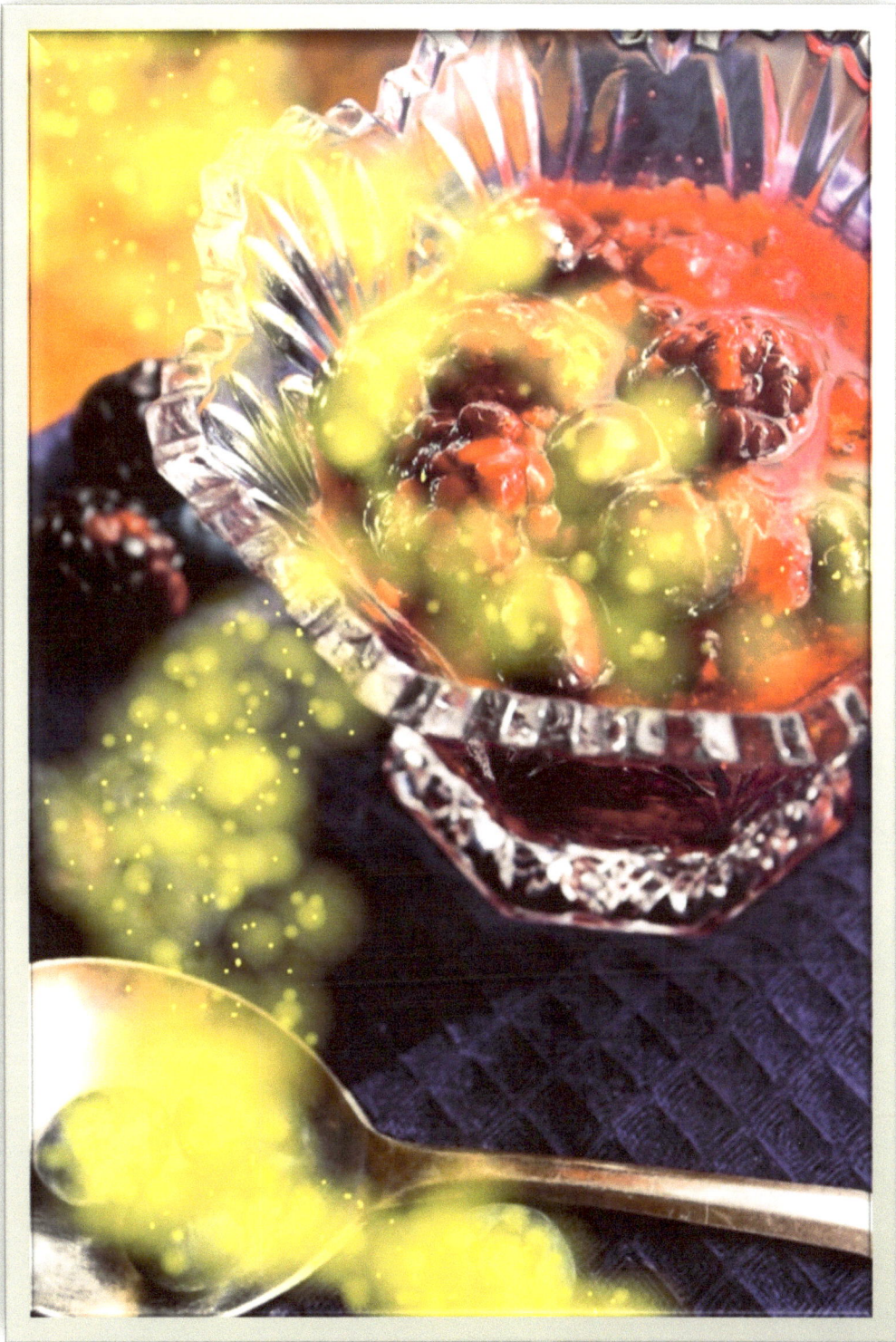

Plum Faery Jam or Jelly

5 Lbs. Plums
2 oz. clear Gelatin (2 packages)
3 1/2 Lbs. Sugar

Leave peelings on for tart, or peel for less tart and de-seed the plums. Put into a pan with a teacup of water. Simmer until tender. Add gelatin, boil for 5 minutes before adding sugar. Then boil for 30 minutes. Bottle. For jelly, after boiling you can sieve all the fruit keeping just the boiled down liquid, and add 4 tsp. of clear gelatin instead of 2 tsp. for a jiggely jelly.

Apple or Plum Butter

5 Lbs. Finely Chopped, peeled and cored Apples
3 1/2 Lbs. White Sugar
4 oz. Butter
2 oz. Cinnamon
1 oz. Nutmeg
½ oz. ground Cloves
2 packages clear Gelatin

Put apples in a pan with a teacup of water. Simmer until tender. Bring to a boil for 5 minutes before adding sugar and gelatin. Then boil well for 30 minutes. Stir in butter, cinnamon, nutmeg, clove at the end. Bottle and store in a cool place. Seal well with air tight canister if you want to keep more than a few months.

Blackberry, Brambleberry or Plum Faery Chutney

1 Gallon Water
1 Pint Malt Vinegar
1oz. Salt
1Lb. Finely Chopped Apples
3 Lbs. Berries or Plums
6 oz. Raisins, chopped
1/2 Lb. Brown Sugar
2 Garlic Cloves, finely minced
1 oz. ground Ginger
1oz. Mustard Seed

Put vinegar and brambleberries, blackberries or pitted cut in half plums in pan and crush. Simmer 30 minutes and sieve. Put with apples, raisins, garlic, spice and salt. Bring to a boil, add sugar and cook for 30 minutes. Stir in a teaspoon of mustard seed. Bottle and store in a dark cool place. Optional: Add a teaspoon of curry powder for a little spicier Faery flavor! Sprinkle with fresh Oregano leaf when serving for an unusual flavor.

Pear Faery Dumpling Muffins

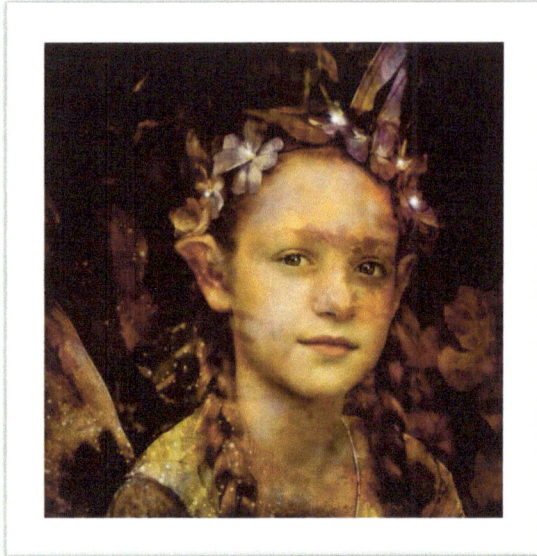

½ Lb. Pears, cored, peeled, finely minced
12 oz. Flour
1 ½ oz. Baking Powder
1 oz. Cinnamon
½ oz. Nutmeg
4 oz. Milk or Cream
4 oz. chopped Walnuts
4 Eggs

Preheat oven to 180˚. Mix all ingredients into a separate bowl, using a wooden spoon or spatula until all the lumps have been smoothed out, adding the pears last. Then, with a large spoon, begin to ladle each dumpling onto a large muffin tin lined with muffin papers. Bake for 12 to 15 minutes until lightly brown on top. Dust the muffins with Confectioner's Powdered Sugar for a simulated Faery dust effect. Enjoy with butter and pear preserves. Or, top off with a dollop of fresh Devonshire Cream.

Pear Faery Preserves

2 Lbs. Pears, cored, peeled, minced
1 Lb. Brown Sugar
1 cube Butter
1 box of Gelatin
2 oz. Cinnamon
1 oz. Nutmeg
Rind of 2 Oranges
Juice of 2 Oranges

In a large saucepan, bring the pears to a boil for five minutes using only half of the butter. Add the rest of the ingredients except the gelatin. Lower the heat, and simmer for approximately 45 minutes. Add your gelatin, stirring constantly for 10 minutes. Spoon the preserves into large canning jars (sterilized with boiling water), and vacuum seal the tops after pouring some canning wax on to each canning jar full of preserves. You can do this whilst the jars are 1/3 immersed in a large pot of water (vacuum seal). When you are finished filling the jars and pouring the wax over top each jar, then turn the pot of water on high, heating up each jar for a couple of minutes. Put each jar top on (do not twist the top on yet, wait until the water is cooled off). When the water is cooled off, the jars will be vacuum packed, and you can then twist the tops on tightly. The preserves will be lovely on top of biscuits, scones and served at your finest English tea parties. Faerielicious!

Pear Raspberry Faery Turnovers

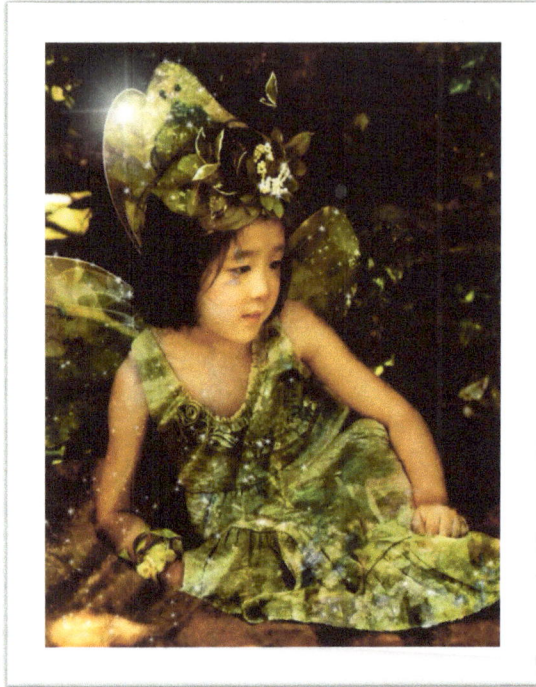

4 cubes Butter
½ Lb. Flour
1 oz. Baking Powder
1 Egg
1 Lb. Pears, cored, peeled, finely chopped
1 Lb. Raspberries
¼ Lb. Sugar
1 oz. Cinnamon
½ oz. Nutmeg
Rind of 1 Orange
2 Tablespoon Lemon juice

Preheat oven to 190° degrees ½ hour before baking. Mix your dough ingredients; Butter, Flour, Baking Powder and Egg, and refrigerate covered in saran wrap for one hour until chilled. Mix all other ingredients into a large saucepan, bring to a boil for five minutes, simmer on low for only ½ hour. Let cool. Roll out your chilled dough onto a well floured surface, cut into individual large squares. Fill the center of each cut out square with the raspberry pear mixture (about one large teaspoon in each) until all the dough has been filled.

Use some melted butter or a beaten egg if you like to brush around the four corners of your dough (working quickly so the dough does not get too soft). Fold over your squares into triangles, and poke the top of each turnover lightly with a fork (allowing ventilation whilst baking). Bake in oven for approximately 12 to 18 minutes until lightly golden brown. Bake less time, if you like a paler turnover crust, and longer for a much richer brown crust. The pear Faery frosting would be lovely on top of each one of these pear turnovers. Serve as dessert or as high tea with Devonshire cream.

Pear Faery Frosting

2 Pears, cored, peeled, and very finely chopped
2 oz. Water
1 oz. Butter
1 oz. Cinnamon
½ oz. Nutmeg
4 oz. Confectioner's Powdered Sugar

In a large saucepan, boil the pears for three to five minutes in ¼ of water, and reduce heat to low. Simmer for approximately 15 minutes. Strain pears through a fine sieve, using your wooden spoon or spatula to push the pears through the fine mesh (or you can use a food processor to puree the mixed cooked pears). Add the rest of your ingredients whilst the pears are still hot, to melt the butter and powdered sugar. Use the frosting to lightly coat cookies, scones, biscuits, muffins, cakes, pastries, turnovers and even fresh fruit or grapes for your English dessert table decoration.

Pear Faery Apple Sauce

2 Lbs. Apples, cored and peeled
2 Lbs. Pears, cored and peeled
Water to cover fruit in Pot
½ Lb. Sugar
2 oz. Cinnamon
½ oz. Nutmeg
2 oz. Lemon juice

In a large pot, boil the apples and pears for ½ hour. Reduce heat to low, and simmer for 1 hour covered. Add the rest of the ingredients to the mixture, and pour through a fine sieve, to remove any lumps. Can or jar the pear apple sauce, and enjoy anytime of the year using a vacuum pack on each canning jar. Sauce is best used when chilled, and used as a separate dish on a table at a fine English tea mid-day. Lovely to pour some heavy cream over top of the sauce, and a fresh sprig of mint to garnish. You may add Peaches instead of apples to this, and make more of a sweet condiment for spooning on scones and biscuits.

Faery Bread and Butter Pudding

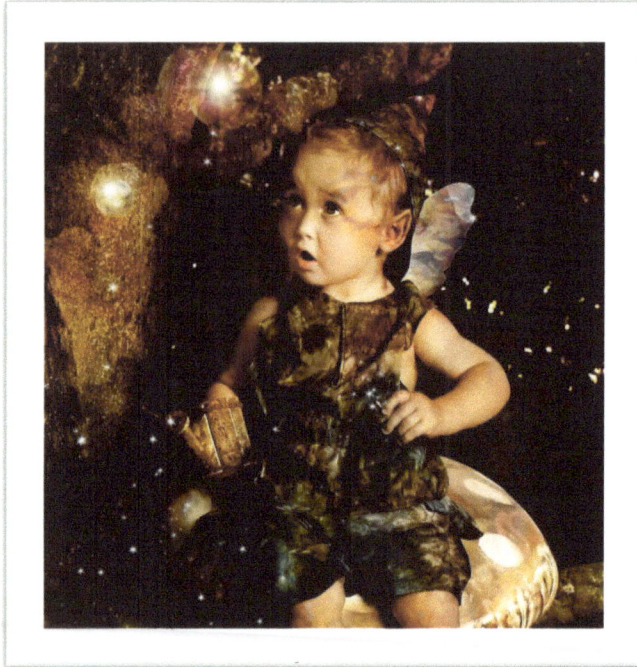

8 oz. Butter
2 oz. granulated Sugar for dusting
1 oz. sifted Sugar
12 slices white Bread, halved
12 slices brown Bread, halved
2 Pints Milk
1 Vanilla Pod
Lemon zest, 3 pieces
1 Lb. Blueberries + ½ Lb. Raisins
2 ounces Candied Peel
Freshly grated Nutmeg to taste
6 Eggs
1 Tablespoon Vanilla Extract
8 full ounces Whipping Cream

Rub 1 oz. of butter around a casserole and dust with 1 tablespoon granulated sugar. Preheat oven to 170°. Butter the bread with the remaining butter. Scald milk in a pan; add the vanilla pod and the lemon zest. Stir in half of the granulated sugar. Increase the heat and dissolve the sugar and then remove from the heat. Arrange some of the cut bread overlapping on the base of the casserole. Sprinkle with some of the blueberries, raisins and candied peel. Place another layer of bread on top - alternating the brown and white slices. Cover with the remaining bread. Sprinkle the remainder of blueberries-raisins on top and grate the nutmeg over them. Break the eggs into a bowl and whisk, slowly stirring into the scalded milk (having removed the lemon zest and vanilla pod). Pour this mixture over the bread. Dust with sugar. Whisk vanilla extract in the whipping cream that you top your pudding with, and refrigerate. Allow the pudding mixture to stand 1 hour. Before placing it in the oven, pour the whipping cream over the pudding. Cook in the preheated 170° oven on the middle shelf for 55 minutes. Top with more whipping cream or ice cream once room temperature and ready to serve (optional).

39

Magical Faeries Trifle

4 Eggs
1 Lb. fine Sugar
2 Lbs. Flour, sifted
Rind of 1/2 Lemon
2 1/2 cups Milk
1 Vanilla Bean
8 Egg Yolks
I Lb. Raspberries, Mixed Berries or Fruit
10 Tablespoons Raspberry Syrup
1 package Gelatin (to make raspberry jelly)
Raspberry juice (a little bit cold and 1 Pint warm, to make Raspberry Jelly)
2 oz. Strawberry Jam
2 oz. blanched Almonds
12 oz. Whipped Cream
2-3 oz. crystallized Fruits (green and red Cherries, Angelicas, and Apricots)
1 oz. toasted Almonds

Preheat oven to 190°. Make sponge cake. Beat eggs and add sugar gradually, beating until combined. Place bowl over hot water and whisk eggs with half of the sugar until thick, light, and larger in volume. Remove bowl from heat and continue to whisk until cool. Fold in sifted flour and lemon rind. Place mixture into an 8-inch cake tin, which has been buttered, sugared and floured, and bake for 30 minutes. Turn onto a rack to cool. To make custard, heat milk with the vanilla bean until boiling. Beat yolks with remaining sugar until thoroughly combined. Pour in hot milk and whisk together. Place custard into saucepan on low heat and stir until thickened. Remove from heat, take out vanilla bean, and allow custard to cool. Assemble trifle. Fill centers of dishes with raspberries. Make raspberry jelly by dissolving the gelatin in a little cold raspberry juice and then combining with warm raspberry juice. Allow to cool. Cut sponge cake in half and then cut one half into eighths. Place 5 slices into the bottom of a crystal bowl and separate each slice with raspberry filling. Pour half of the raspberry syrup over the cake and then pour over the raspberry jelly. Cut the 3 remaining pieces of cake into thin slices and lay on top. Place into the refrigerator to set. When the jelly has set, smear with the strawberry jam and scatter the blanched almonds over the top. Cover with the cooled custard and place in the refrigerator to set for 1 hour. Decorate trifle with whipped cream Keep in the refrigerator. Yum!

Faery Mincemeat Pie

2 pounds puff Pastry
1 Lb. cooked Sweet Potatoes, skins removed, cooled
1 Lb. Macintosh Apples, peeled and cored
2 oz. dark Brown Sugar
1 oz. Molasses
4 oz. Apple Cider
1 oz. Cinnamon
1 oz. Mace
1 oz. ground Ginger
½ oz. ground Cloves
1 oz. Nutmeg
4 oz. Frangelico or Amaretto (can use extract)
3 oz. dried Currants
3 oz. Raisins
3 oz. Citron
4 oz. Walnuts
3 navel Oranges, cut in paper thin rounds

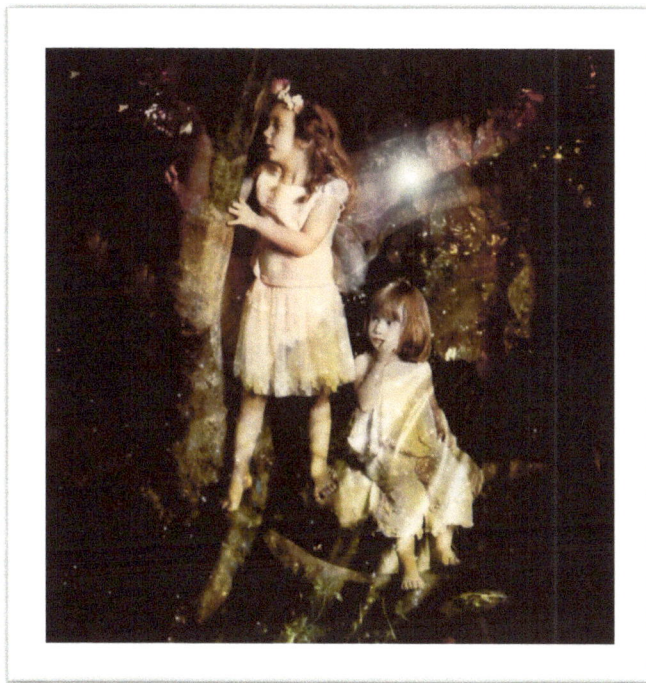

Preheat oven to 225°. Cut puff pastry into 4-inch squares and fit into fluted individual tartlet pans or brioche tartlet tins. Cover with parchment and fill with pie weights, or beans. Bake 12 to 14 minutes or until golden brown. Remove from oven. Lift out parchment and weights and cool tartlets on a rack. Place the sweet potato pulp in a food processor. Add the apples and pulse until coarse. Add the sugar, molasses, cider, cinnamon, mace, ginger, cloves, nutmeg and Frangelico or Amaretto and pulse to combine. Fold in the currants, raisins, citron and walnuts. Pour equal amounts of the filling into baked tartlet shells and refrigerate. On a non-stick cookie sheet, lay out orange slices and sprinkle with sugar. Dry in 225° oven for about 7 minutes or until caramelized. Garnish tartlets with whipped cream and orange slices.

Faery Good Carrot Cake

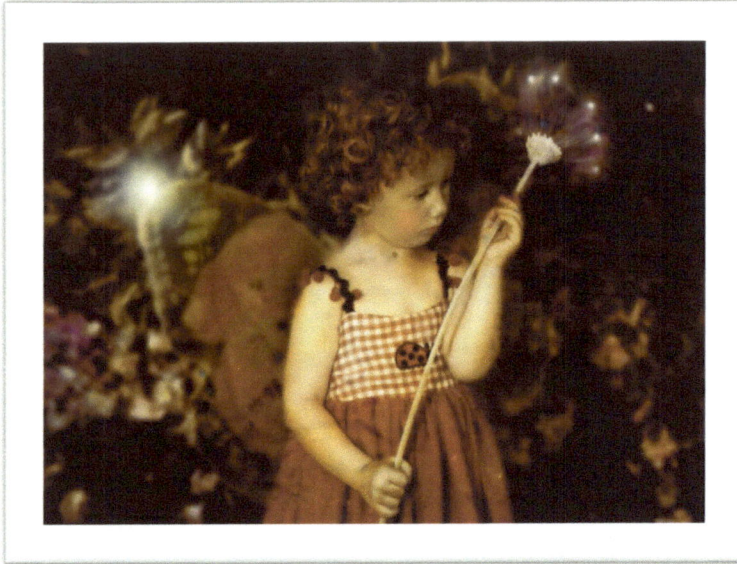

1 Lb. granulated Sugar
10 oz. Hazelnuts
3 1/2 oz. sultana Raisins
3 medium Carrots (10 ounces)
6 Egg yolks
6 Egg whites
1 oz. cold water
2 pinches Freshly ground Salt
2 oz. Lemon Juice
1 oz. Lemon zest (thin rind)
1 ½ Lbs. All Purpose Flour
1 oz. teaspoon Cinnamon
4 oz. Raspberry Jam
4 oz. Icing Sugar

Sift the granulated sugar. Crush the hazelnuts very small (best results in a blender). Wash the sultanas. Wash and grate the carrots. Grease the 2 cake tins (25 x 5 cm.) with a pat of butter. Place a bowl over a pan of hot water. Preheat oven to 180°. Into a warmed bowl place the egg yolks and half of the granulated sugar and whisk together until the mixture thickens. (It should be doubled in bulk, lighter in color and creamy in texture). When this happens, set aside the yolk and sugar mixture for a moment (off the heat). Into a clean, cold bowl place the whites of eggs, add cold water and some freshly ground salt and whisk quickly until they are stiff and peaked. Gradually beat into the fluffy whites of eggs the remaining granulated sugar until it is fully incorporated. Set aside. Place the egg yolk mixture over the warm water and add the ground nuts and lemon juice. To this add the grated carrots and lemon zest. Fold in the 1 teaspoonful of flour and sultanas. Remove the bowl from the heated water. Fold in egg yolks. Then put all the mixture into the remainder of the whites of eggs and fold in well. Add the cinnamon. Pour all the mixture into the greased cake tin and put it into the preheated oven set at 180°., on the middle shelf, for 60 minutes. Remove cake from the pan and cool completely. Cut cake in half, spread the jam over the bottom and replace top. Sprinkle with confectioners' sugar before serving.

Faery Celebration Cake

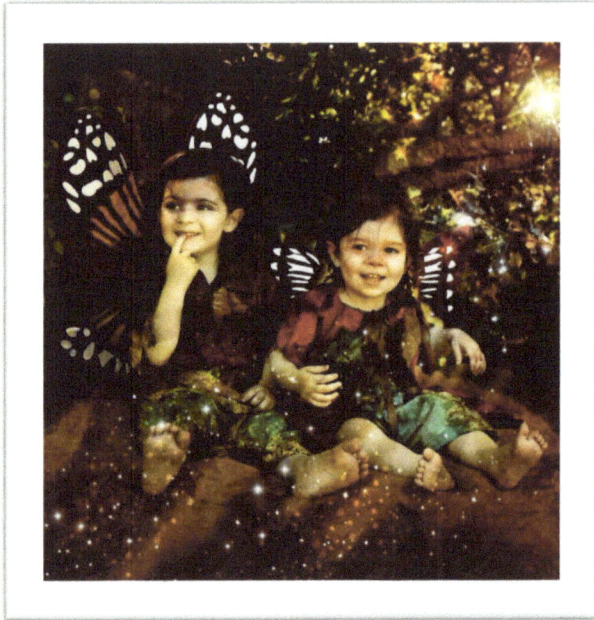

1 Lb. Strawberries or Currants
½ Lb. Sugar
 8 full ounces Water
8 full ounces dry Sherry
1 recipe Basic Sponge Cake (recipe follows)
4 oz. toasted slivered Almonds (optional)
1 recipe Crème Anglaise (recipe follows)
8 full ounces Sweetened Whipped Cream
12 fresh Mint sprigs (optional)

In a medium-size saucepan over medium heat, combine the currants, sugar, and water. Bring to a boil and cook for 10 minutes. Remove from the heat and stir in the sherry. Let cool completely. Spread the mixture evenly over the sponge cake, and then sprinkle the almonds evenly over the strawberries. Spoon over the whipped cream, and garnish with a mint sprig.

BASIC SPONGE CAKE

2 oz. Milk
35 ml. unsalted Butter
8 large Eggs
8 full ounces Sugar
4 oz. bleached All Purpose Flour
1 oz. Baking Powder
Pinch of Salt
1 oz. pure Vanilla Extract

Preheat the oven to 180°. In a small saucepan, warm the milk and butter together over medium-low heat. With an electric mixer fitted with a wire whip, beat the eggs and the sugar on medium-high speed until the mixture is pale yellow and thick, and has tripled in volume, about 8 minutes. With the mixer on low, beat in the warm milk mixture. Sift the flour, baking powder, and salt into a medium-size mixing bowl. Fold the flour mixture into the egg mixture and blend thoroughly until smooth. Add the vanilla and mix gently with a spatula. Grease a 25 x 5 cm round baking pan or jellyroll pan with a pat of butter. Sprinkle evenly with a fine dusting of sugar. Pour the batter into the pan, spreading it evenly. Bake until the cake springs back when touched, about 15 minutes. Cool for about 2 minutes, and then gently flip it out onto a large wire rack or a large sheet of parchment paper. Let cool completely. This recipe will make 1 sponge cake.

CREME ANGLAISE for Sponge Cake:

5 large Egg yolks + 4 oz. Sugar
Three-quarters of a pint heavy Cream
1 oz. pure Vanilla Extract

Put the yolks in a saucepan and add the sugar. Beat with a wire whisk until thick and lemon colored. Put the cream in a non-reactive saucepan and heat to the scalding point (when bubbles form around the edge of the pan). Gradually add the cream to the yolk mixture, beating constantly. Cook over low heat until the mixture thickens slightly. Do not overcook or boil, as the sauce will curdle. Remove from the heat and stir in the vanilla. Strain through a fine-mesh sieve into a cold bowl. Cover with plastic wrap, pressing it down on the surface to prevent a skin from forming if not using immediately.

My Faery's Favorite Shortbread

8 ounces (2 sticks) butter, room temperature
1 Lb. Sugar
8 oz. Flour
2 oz. Cornstarch
4 oz. Water
1 oz. salted Butter
4 oz. heavy Cream, heated to lukewarm
8 ounces semisweet Chocolate
1 oz. Grapeseed Oil
Zest from 1 Lemon (Optional)

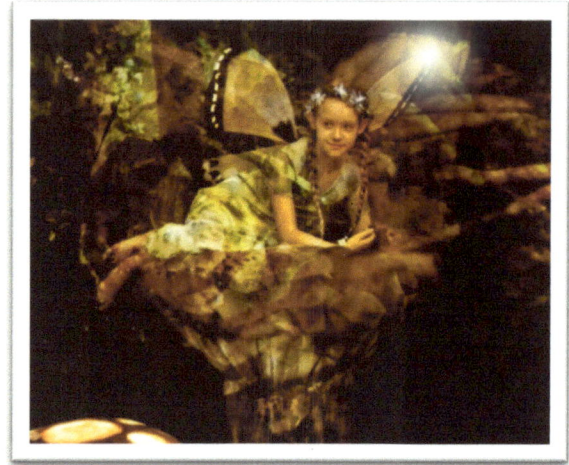

Preheat the oven to 190°. Line a 25 x 5 cm. baking pan with parchment or grease with a pat of butter. In a mixer fitted with a paddle attachment (or using a hand mixer), cream the butter until soft. Add half of the sugar and mix until incorporated. In a separate bowl, stir together the flour and cornstarch. Add the dry ingredients to the butter mixture and mix at low speed just until the ingredients are incorporated and the dough comes together. Turn the dough onto a floured work surface and knead it 5 to 10 times, to bring the dough together and smooth it out. Re-flour your work surface. With a rolling pin, roll the dough out to fit the sheet pan. To transfer to the sheet pan, roll the dough up onto the rolling pin, lift it up, unroll into the pan or use cookie cutters to make cookies. Using light strokes of the rolling pin, roll the dough into the corners and edges of the pan, and roll out any bumps (or press the rolled-out dough thoroughly into the pan with your fingers). Prick the shortbread all over with a fork to prevent any buckling or shrinking. Bake in the center of the oven for 15 minutes. After 15 minutes, rotate the pan and knock it once against the oven rack, to ensure even cooking and a flat surface. Bake 10 to 15 minutes more, until very lightly browned. Let cool in the pan. Pour the remaining half of the sugar into the center of a deep saucepan. Carefully pour the water around the sugar, trying not to splash any sugar onto the sides of the pan. Do not stir; gently draw your finger through the center of the sugar twice, making a cross, to moisten it. Over medium-high heat, bring to a boil without stirring. Reduce the heat to a fast simmer and cook without stirring until amber-caramel in color, 10 to 20 minutes. Immediately remove from the heat and stir in the butter with a wooden spoon. Slowly pour in the lukewarm cream, stirring slowly but constantly (it will bubble up and may splatter). Pour over the baked shortbread and smooth the top. Faery delicious!

Place in the refrigerator, uncovered, to harden slightly. When the caramel has set, melt the chocolate in the top of a double boiler (or in a mixing bowl) set over barely simmering water, stirring frequently. Stir in the grapeseed oil (this will make the chocolate less brittle when it hardens). Pour over the cooled caramel and spread quickly with the back of a spatula or spoon to cover the entire surface. Let cool in the pan. With a heavy knife, cut into bars. Or, if you prefer, you can pre-cut dough into cookie cutter shapes of your choice before baking and set aside the chocolate to pour over the cookies when dessert is served to your guests. Store in an air tight container.

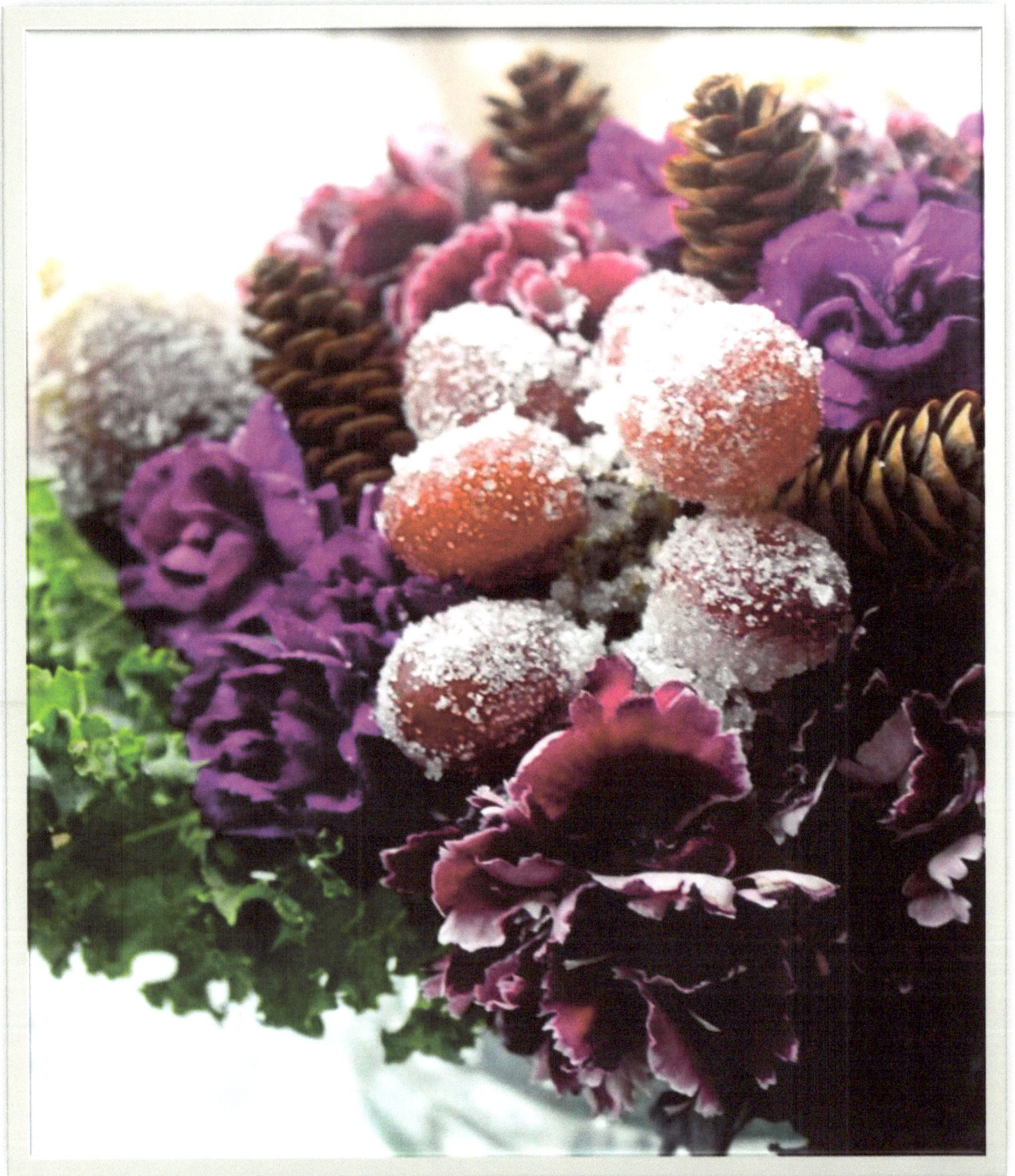

Sugar Faery Dust Plums

24 Large Plums
6 oz. Honey
8 oz. Organic Sugar (coarse)
2 oz. White Powdered Sugar as Faery Dust (optional)

Coat the Plums with the warmed honey in a large mixing bowl, mixing gently. Put wax paper on two large baking sheets, and begin to place the Plums individually on the cooking sheet (or wax paper) spacing them out 4 cm. apart from each other. Dust the Plums with Faery Dust and Sugar. Allow to dry, and place on a serving platter during a decadent Faery feast or during your exquisite Faery tea party!

Sugar Plum Faery Dreams

Sugar Plums shimmer

Dusted with White...

The Sugar Sprinkles,

Faery Dust Light-

Achooo!

A Faery nose crinkles...

For Sugar Plum Dreams

A Faery Good Night-

Faery Universe

The Faery Universe IS

In ALL of its Existence

Whether we be HERE and NOW...

Or see that of a Rainbow

Coming out of a CLOUD

Faeries unseen

Light and Breath Redeem

All Qualities

Of a Faery UNIVERSE

UNSEEN

Faery Delight Universe

Love your Faeries!

Health Conscious Recipe Ingredient Substitutes

For those who want to cook and bake with healthy ingredients, you can use the following ingredients as recipe ingredient replacement(s);

Buttermilk – Yogurt and Tofu Milk or Rice Dream, mix until the consistency is like Buttermilk (good for the digestive tract).

Chocolate – Sugar Free Dark Chocolate Chips or Organic Carob Chips (and add 1 oz. extra Chicolin sweetener to this for a richer flavor).

Eggs – Substitute Vegan Ener-G Egg replacer or Egg Beaters.

Milk – Non-Dairy Tofu Milk or Rice Dream (Vanilla or Plain).

Whipped Cream – Whip Firm 6 oz. Tofu with 2 oz. Egg Replacement until fluffy and add 1 oz. Rice Dream, Silk or Tofu Milk.

White Flour – White Spelt Flour, Quinoa Flour, Almond Flour, All Purpose Gluten Free Flour (wheat-free for baking, use the lighter version of this flour), and Rice Flour (for Celiac disease).

White Sugar – Agave Nectar, Sugar in the Raw, Light Brown Sugar, Honey or Chicolin (a natural sweetener that is for diabetics, and produces natural "inulin" in the digestive tract).

Faery Recipes INDEX

Faery Recipes INDEX

About the Author

Linda Larson writes children's Faerytales, and a recipe cook book all good Faeries will enjoy in the kitchen with their extended Spriten spirit family members and friends. Linda is an alchemist in the kitchen while concocting very tasty Quinoa Fusion Recipes and Gourmet Cooking tips with her readers while introducing them to the world of healthy food alternatives for energetic lifestyles. Although, she spends a great deal of time writing and publishing, her most important priority is her love of sharing joy-filled Faerytale stories for children, cook books and whole food cooking methods with people around the world. Linda's goal is to introduce healthy cooking with organic foods to as many people as possible.

Linda is excited to share the promotion of easy to cook meals incorporating whole foods and healthy gourmet lifestyle and has over 23 Certifications in the profession of Ancient Healing Arts to locations such as; China, Japan, Turkey, U.K. and Ireland.

Her Culinary Healing Arts endeavors have far reached around the world to many people's families, friends and children with a vision to assist the healing of each person's body, mind, spirit and to be fun inspired where these products are meant to also excite the palate.

Body, Mind & Spirit: Linda studies and practices meditation and prayer. She loves art, music, movies, whole foods, Faerytale stories, all animals, horseback riding, organic farming, agriculture, gourmet cooking, creating yummy recipes and extraordinary culinary adventures.

For more information, please visit: www.Fae Entertainment.ca

www.ingramcontent.com/pod-product-compliance
Lightning Source LLC
Chambersburg PA
CBHW060824090426
42738CB00003B/101